CLARA BARTON
Angel of the Battlefield

By the Editors of TIME For Kids
WITH ANNA PROKOS

Collins
An Imprint of HarperCollins*Publishers*

About the Author: In fifth grade, Anna Prokos wrote a profile of Clara Barton and has been a fan ever since. The author lives in New Jersey with her husband and two children.

Collins is an imprint of HarperCollins Publishers.
Clara Barton
Copyright © 2008 by Time Inc.
Used under exclusive license by HarperCollins Publishers Inc.
Manufactured in China.

Library of Congress Cataloging-in-Publication Data is available.
ISBN 978-0-06-057622-6 (pbk). — ISBN 978-0-06-057623-3 (trade)

2 3 4 5 6 7 8 9 10
First Edition

Copyright © by Time Inc.

TIME FOR KIDS and the Red Border Design are Trademarks of Time Inc. used under license.

Photography and Illustration Credits:
Cover: The Granger Collection; cover background: The Library of Congress; cover inset: American Red Cross; title page: The National Park Service; contents page: The National Park Service; p. iv: The Library of Congress; p. 1: MPI-Hulton Archive-Getty Images; p. 2: Bettmann-Corbis; p. 3: Bettmann-Corbis; p. 4: AP Photo-Michael Dwyer; p. 5: The Granger Collection; p. 6: Jeffrey Coolidge-Corbis; p. 7 (top): Corbis; p. 7 (bottom): courtesy of the Clara Barton Birthplace Museum; p. 8 (top): courtesy of the Clara Barton Birthplace Museum; p. 8 (bottom): The Granger Collection; p. 10: The Granger Collection; p. 11: The National Park Service; p. 12: The Granger Collection; p. 13: The Granger Collection; p. 14: The National Park Service; p. 15: The Granger Collection; p. 16: courtesy of the Fort Plain Free Library, NY, and the Mohawk Valley Library System, NY; p. 17: Bettmann-Corbis; p. 18: The Granger Collection; p. 19: Hulton Archive-Corbis; p. 20: The Granger Collection; p. 21 (top): Picture History; p. 21 (bottom): Medford Historical Collection-Corbis; p. 22: Bettmann-Corbis; p. 23: MPI-Hulton Archive-Getty Images; p. 24: The Library of Congress; p. 25 (top): Corbis; p. 26: Picture History; p. 27 (top): The Library of Congress; p. 27 (bottom): Alex Peck Medical Antiques; p. 28 (top): The Library of Congress; p. 28 (bottom): The Granger Collection; p. 29: March of Time-Time Life Pictures-Getty Images; p. 30: AP Photo-General Services Administration; p. 31: The Granger Collection; p. 32: Raymond Gehman Collection; p. 33: Bettmann-Corbis; p. 34: The Granger Collection; p. 35: Bettmann-Corbis; p. 36: The National Park Service; p. 37: American Red Cross; p. 38: The National Park Service; p. 39: The Library of Congress; p. 40: Corbis; p. 41: Northwind; p. 42: American Red Cross; p. 43 (top): AP Photo-Tom Hood; p. 43 (bottom): American Red Cross; p. 44 (top): Library of Congress; p. 44 (middle): The Granger Collection; p. 44 (middle): The Library of Congress; p. 44 (bottom): Corbis; back cover: The National Park Service

Acknowledgments:
For TIME FOR KIDS: Designer: Colleen Pidel; Photography Editors: Sandy Perez Sanchez and Jon Protas

go **Find out more at www.timeforkids.com/bio/barton**

30092000142479   4/08

CONTENTS

"While our soldiers can stand and fight, I can stand and feed and nurse them."

—CLARA BARTON

Chapter 1

Clara Risks Her LIFE

It was a hot afternoon in August 1862. Clara Barton had traveled for two days from Washington, D.C., to reach Culpeper, Virginia. Shocked and frightened, she looked out onto the Civil War battlefield. Foul-smelling smoke from guns and cannons burned her eyes. She saw dead and wounded soldiers lying on the ground. They had been there for days. But Clara didn't allow fear to stand in her way. Her nursing was desperately needed. She rushed to the soldiers and handed them food, water, and fresh clothing. Clara held the outstretched hands of dying men. She wrote

▲ CIVIL WAR battles were bloody as Americans fought against fellow Americans.

down messages for their families. The brave nurse made and tied bandages for the soldiers and helped doctors clean wounds. Hardly ever resting, Clara was busy day and night caring for the men. Working in the worst of conditions, she thought only of others. Her strength and courage kept her going.

A Civil War battlefield was a dangerous place to be. Women were told to stay away. In the 1800s, they were expected to remain home, caring for their families. But Clara had no husband or children. The soldiers were like her family. When friends tried to talk her out of going to the battlefields, Clara would tell them, "My place is anywhere between the bullet and the hospital." She was not afraid to risk her life to help the hurt and wounded.

At first, Clara only treated soldiers on the Union side. (The

◄ INJURED SOLDIERS wait for help on a Civil War battlefield.

▶ UNION soldiers take a badly needed rest after a battle.

Union was fighting against the Confederacy, which wanted to keep slavery.) But as she helped the wounded men, she realized that every soldier needed care. "Pain and suffering don't take sides," Clara said. So she tried to help any soldier in need, black or white, Union or Confederate.

Clara's nursing experience led to the most lasting achievement of her life. After the Civil War, she started the American Red Cross, an organization that helps people during times of war and natural disaster. How did Clara become such a brave and caring woman who made an important difference in people's lives? Part of the answer can be found in events that happened in Clara's life while she was growing up.

Chapter 2

Growing Up SMART

On a cold Christmas night in 1821, Stephen Barton left his warm farmhouse in North Oxford, Massachusetts, to find a doctor. His wife, Sarah, was about to have a baby. By the time he returned, the cries of a newborn child echoed through the Barton home. They named the baby Clarissa Harlowe Barton— Clara, for short.

Clara was the youngest of five children. Her two older sisters,

◀ VISITORS can go to Clara Barton's childhood home, which still stands today.

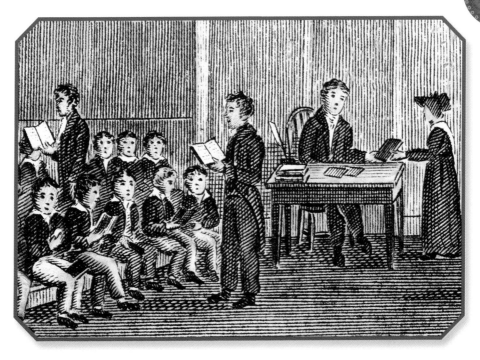

▲ COUNTRY SCHOOLS were often one room, crowded, and had benches instead of desks.

Dorothea and Sally, often looked after her. They liked teaching Clara how to read and write. They also taught her geography. Her oldest brother, Stephen, helped her with math. Her other brother, David, showed Clara how to ride and care for a horse.

Star Student

Clara was four years old when she started school. Like many kids, she was nervous on her first day. The one-room schoolhouse was crowded with nearly one hundred students of all ages. Clara felt out of place. She was shorter than the other children, and she was also a bit heavy. Clara's thick brown hair was cut very short in an old-fashioned style. The other girls stared at her plain green dress. The older boys made fun of her lisp and how she mispronounced words.

But Clara impressed her teacher on her first day of school. She could solve tough math problems and spell *artichoke* too. And she could point out countries and cities on maps. Clara liked learning new things. She was an excellent and curious student.

Learning About Life

After school, Clara would sit on her father's lap and listen to his stories about the army. Captain Stephen Barton had fought in the Indian Wars during the late 1700s. He taught Clara about the importance of serving her country and helping others. It was a lesson that Clara learned at a very early age—and it would stay with her forever.

Clara also learned many important lessons from her mother. Sarah Barton believed that women should have the same rights as men—such as the right to vote, which women couldn't do back then. Sarah talked to her children about equal treatment for all people. She taught her daughters how to do "men's work," such as chopping wood. She believed women should be prepared for anything that came their way.

▼ **STEPHEN BARTON** taught Clara about the importance of helping others.

Clara grew up in a time when women did not have equal rights with men.

- Women could not vote.
- If a couple divorced, men generally got legal control of the children and all property.
- States could bar women from certain professions, such as medicine and law.
- Even when they held the same jobs as men, women were paid much less than men.

In 1848, about 300 women met in Seneca Falls, New York, to bring attention to these problems. This was the beginning of the movement to win equal rights for women in the United States.

Growing up, Clara learned about the importance of loyalty to her country, and to family and friends, from her father. She learned about the importance of standing up for her beliefs from her mother. And from the loving way her siblings treated her, she learned how to care for others. These lessons helped shape Clara throughout her life.

Friends on the Farm

The Bartons moved to a bigger farm in North Oxford when Clara was eight. Now she had lots of room to ride her horse, Billy. Like most farm kids, Clara had chores to do. She milked the cows and fed the ducks, chickens, and lambs. She also cared for injured and sick animals, a job she took very seriously. Clara learned how to be responsible and understood that hard work was important.

When she wasn't busy on the farm, Clara liked to play. Sometimes she would visit with her cousins, Otis and Jerry. The boys wanted to teach Clara how to ice-skate, but her parents didn't want her to. They said she might get hurt. Clara disagreed. So one winter night, the kids snuck out of their houses. The boys tied a blanket around Clara's waist. One cousin pulled the blanket from the front, while the other skated next to Clara to help her balance. All was well until they hit a patch of thin, cracked ice—and Clara fell on the sharp edges. When her parents saw her cuts, they knew she had disobeyed them. Clara was punished for weeks.

Besides skating, Clara also explored caves, climbed trees, and chased snakes. She was athletic and strong. Even as a young child, she showed an independent spirit that would remain with her all her life.

▼ THIS is a typical New England family farm from the mid-1800s.

Chapter 3

A Very Young
NURSE

Tragedy struck the Barton family when Clara was eleven. Clara's brother David was building a barn. As he worked on the roof, a rafter snapped from under him. David fell, landing hard on his feet. Days later he came down with a headache and fever. The doctor didn't know what was wrong. David was ordered to bed, where he mostly stayed for two years.

Since David was too weak to care for himself,

▼ BARNS housed animals and farm supplies.

Clara became his nurse. She brought him food, water, and medicine. But even so, David grew weaker. With Clara's excellent caring and a good diet, David finally got better.

Clara enjoyed nursing David and she liked taking care of people. So she looked for different ways to help anyone in need.

Clara to the Rescue

Once Clara turned thirteen, mothers often asked her to babysit their children. She didn't make much money though, because many of the families were poor. When they needed money, Clara asked her father to give them some. She

▶ CARING for others was important to young Clara.

▲ BABYSITTING was one way women earned some extra money.

also educated needy families, teaching the kids how to read and write. Clara found great pleasure in improving their lives.

A few years later, Clara's nursing skills came in handy when a severe illness swept through her town. Clara prepared healthy dinners for sick people. She gave patients cups of tea and comforted them.

The Barton family was proud of Clara, but they wanted her to spend more time with people her own age. Sarah Barton asked a phrenologist named L. N. Fowler to help her daughter. (A phrenologist was someone who believed that different parts of the brain control different behaviors. This science is hardly ever practiced today.) Fowler believed that you could tell a lot about someone's personality and talents by the shape and size of the head. So after examining Clara's head, he uttered the words that would influence the next few years of Clara's life. "She has all the qualities of a teacher!" he exclaimed. Clara would soon take him up on his suggestion.

▶ PHRENOLOGISTS thought that the shape of the head determined thoughts, feelings, and actions.

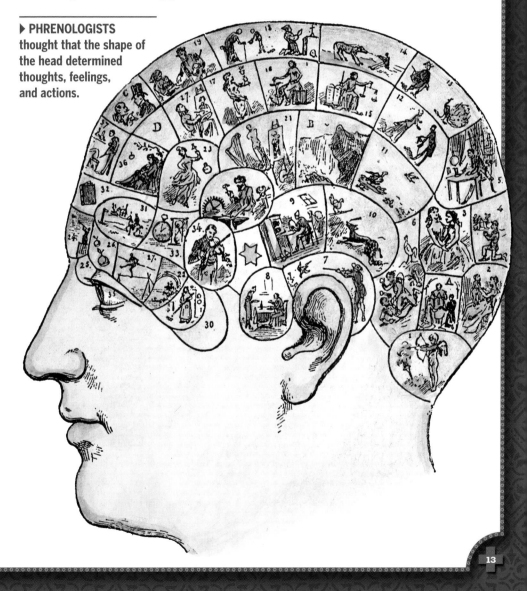

Chapter 4

An Excellent
TEACHER

With no training, Clara started teaching summer school in 1839, when she was seventeen. Some of the older students were about her age. She worried that they wouldn't listen to her, but was surprised when they paid attention.

Clara gained the respect of some of her students by challenging them in the classroom. But she gained the respect of her rowdier boys at recess. When they realized how well she could

◄ **CLARA** was only seventeen when she began teaching.

▲ A LOG made a perfect base for a seesaw—a popular activity in the 1800s.

throw a ball, they changed their rough behavior. Soon Miss Barton became known as the best teacher in North Oxford.

The heads of nearby schools heard about Clara's success with her students. They wanted her to teach summer classes at their schools too. One year, Clara was asked to teach the winter session, which was usually only taught by male teachers. Clara was excited—until school officials explained that her salary would be lower than the men's salaries. Then she was insulted. "I may sometimes be willing to teach for nothing," she told them, "but if paid at all, I shall never do a man's work for less than a man's pay." It was a bold statement for a woman to make at that time. But school officials changed their minds and paid her the same salary as they paid male teachers.

Clara Goes to School

Even though Clara was a terrific teacher, she wanted a new challenge. So she left North Oxford and became a student at a school for female educators in Clinton, New York. When she graduated in 1851, Clara moved in with friends in Hightstown, New Jersey. She found a job teaching at a private school there. However, Clara was upset because New Jersey did not have a free public school system for all children. She wanted to change that. So Clara decided to start a school in nearby Bordentown. It took two years to build the school, collect the books, and attract

▼ CLARA went to the Liberal Institute in Clinton, New York, where she studied math, science, German, and French.

students. Finally, Clara's dream came true. Her free public school had more than two hundred students.

Bordentown realized that having a public school would be a good idea. So they raised money for a new school that would be big enough to fit the six hundred students who had enrolled by 1854.

Even though Clara had started the school, officials decided to hire a man to lead it. Clara was angry. After all her hard work, she felt she should be in charge. So she decided it was time to quit teaching. Clara was ready for a new career and a move to a new city.

The First TEXTBOOK

When William McGuffey was a young teacher in the 1820s, he used reading and spelling books from the 1700s in his school. The material was very old, and the children were bored. So McGuffey decided to write his own reading and spelling books.

MCGUFFEY'S FIRST READER.

LESSON I.

can   has   the   read   John   name
her   two   that   keep   book   there
see   you   with   Jane   hand   clean
boy   how   girls   they   must   learn

Do you see that boy?
There are two girls with him.
The name of the boy is John.
Jane has a book in her hand.
They can all read from the book.
They must keep the book clean.
They must see how fast they can learn.

His books, later called *McGuffey's Readers*, helped to change public education in the United States. The readers, first published in 1836, had many kinds of stories that students enjoyed. The books also taught children how to live honest and decent lives. Over time, the readers would become the most used textbooks in the United States. McGuffey's readers were so popular, versions of them were in classrooms for more than ninety years!

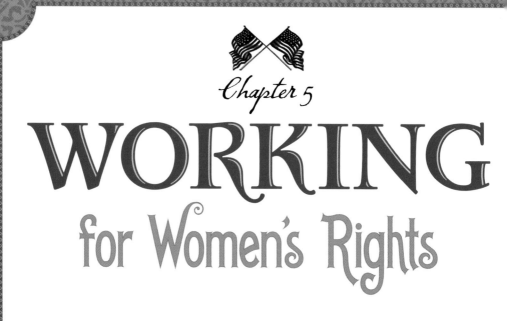

Chapter 5

WORKING
for Women's Rights

Clara's search for new challenges led her to Washington, D.C. She found a job with the U.S. Patent Office, where every new invention is registered. As a clerk, Clara hand-copied patent applications. She was happy and she liked her work.

In 1855 a new person was named to run the Patent Office. He thought that since women were not allowed to vote, they shouldn't be able to work for the government either. So Clara and the other

◀CLARA spent her days copying patents by hand. (Remember, this was before copying machines!)

▲ **BARTON** often visited the U.S. Capitol to hear debates about new laws. The dome was built in the late 1850s.

female clerks were fired. Clara didn't go quietly, however. She asked her family and friends to write letters to the government. After a few months, Clara was given her job back. She was now the only female clerk working at the Patent Office.

The men at the office made Clara's life difficult. When she went to work each morning, they would make fun of her and treat her rudely. At that time many men believed women belonged at home. Clara worked hard to prove them wrong. On one occasion, she did two weeks' worth of work in only six days. Her fingers were sore from writing so much. Clara put up with these hard conditions until 1857, when her position was eliminated.

Instead of trying to stay at the Patent Office in another position, Clara returned to North Oxford and tried to find work there. But she missed her government job and her friends in the nation's capital. She didn't know what to do. Clara visited her old doctor, L. N. Fowler, and asked for advice. He told her to get some rest, then try to find work.

When the Patent Office called her to work again in November 1860, Clara was ready to return to Washington, D.C. She started copying patent

▼ THIS WAS A TYPICAL KITCHEN in the 1800s. Many men believed that women belonged here, instead of in the workplace.

applications immediately. There were a few women working at the office, and the men still didn't treat them very nicely. But this time Clara was determined to stay. The best way to do that, she believed, was to meet important people who might help her keep her job. She quickly became friends with Henry Wilson, a senator from Massachusetts, Clara's home state.

▲ L. N. FOWLER advised Clara to rest and relax.

Wilson was also good friends with Abraham Lincoln, who had just become president. Clara asked Wilson to talk to the president about keeping women in government jobs. Lincoln agreed with Clara. He assured her that she would always have her job at the Patent Office.

Lincoln's decision made Clara feel hopeful. She believed she was paving the way for all women to work for the government. Clara was more convinced than ever that women should be treated equally with men.

▶ SENATOR HENRY WILSON and Clara Barton became good friends.

Chapter 6

Clara Heads to WAR

It was April 12, 1861, a typical Friday at work for Clara—but not for long. Clara, like so many Americans, was upset to hear that the Confederate army fired at Fort Sumter in Charleston, South Carolina. The Union troops had been placed there to protect the fort. Cannons and gunfire blasted for thirty-six hours. Finally, the Union troops gave up.

▼ **THE FIRST** shots of the Civil War took place at Fort Sumter.

One week later, President Lincoln asked for 75,000 volunteers to help protect Washington, D.C., from the battles that were sure to follow. Troops

▲ **MANY UNION SOLDIERS** were wounded or killed by Baltimore residents.

from the North arrived in Baltimore, Maryland, on their way to the nation's capital. Most people in Baltimore were in favor of the South. When they saw the northern soldiers stepping off the train, the Baltimore mobs attacked them. Many soldiers were injured; others were killed. The soldiers were then taken by train to nearby Washington, D.C. Clara went to the station with her sister Sally, who had recently moved to the capital.

The first soldiers to get off the train were from Massachusetts. Clara was shocked to see that forty of them were her former students. And the young soldiers were hurt and scared.

Clara Makes a Difference

Since there was no room in the small hospital for the soldiers, Clara and Sally took matters into their own hands. They brought many of the hurt men to Sally's nearby house. The women listened to the soldiers' stories. Most of them had no clothes left except for what they were wearing. Many had not eaten in days.

That night, Clara packed up thread, scissors, sheets, handkerchiefs, and anything else she thought the soldiers would need. The next morning, she used her own money to buy food, clothing, and other goods. She put everything in big baskets and hired people to carry them to the Senate building. Many soldiers were staying there until they could be moved to another place. The troops were happy to see Clara. They ate the food she had brought and changed into the clean clothes. From then on, Clara knew she had a mission. "So far as our poor efforts can reach," she said, the soldiers "shall never lack a kindly hand or a

▼ **DURING THE CIVIL WAR,** eleven hospitals were built in Washington, D.C., to care for wounded troops.

24

▲ **SALLY BARTON**
helped her sister care
for wounded troops.

sister's sympathy."

Clara asked her friends and neighbors to sew clothes for the troops. Soon women from around the country were sending Clara honey, soap, lemons, pickled fruits, clothing, and other items the soldiers needed. Food and supplies kept pouring in. Clara held the boxes in her one-room apartment until she ran out of space. Then she rented a warehouse to store all the items. Six months later, Clara's supplies filled *three* warehouses!

Clara decided to take everything directly to the soldiers on the battlefields. But getting there wasn't easy. Women usually weren't allowed near the fighting. But when Clara told an army officer about the supplies she

had collected, he was impressed. The officer gave her a pass for six wagons, men to help her load them, and a pass to get to the front lines of the battlefield. Finally, Clara got what she wanted—the chance to help people who needed her the most.

At the Front Lines

Clara's first stop was the Union camps in Fredericksburg, Virginia, on August 3, 1862. She handed out supplies and food. She comforted the troops. They all were very grateful for Clara's help.

On August 9, Clara heard news of the Battle of

Civil War

◄ HUNDREDS of thousands of soldiers were injured during the Civil War. More than 600,000 died.

Besides the fear of getting killed in the Civil War, soldiers were mostly frightened of being treated by doctors who worked in filthy conditions.

Just one look at a doctor's bag was enough to make any soldier nervous. At best, there would be saws, pliers, clamps, and knives of all sizes. If a doctor didn't have the right medical equipment, he would stick his fingers in the wound and poke around until he was able to get the bullet out.

About three out of five

Cedar Mountain in Culpeper, Virginia. Nearly 2,000 soldiers were badly wounded or killed there. Clara and two helpers headed with their wagons to Culpeper. As Clara worked, she noted the name of each soldier in her pocket diary. At the request of the soldiers, she wrote messages to their families. The soldiers

MEDICINE

soldiers who died in the Civil War died from disease. One reason was that doctors didn't know how to sterilize, or clean, their medical equipment. They also went for days without washing their hands because there was a shortage of water. There wasn't even enough water to flush out slop pits, or toilets. The conditions were so awful that soldiers went to the bathroom right outside the hospital. This spread illnesses even further. Also, bacteria got

▶ A CIVIL WAR medical kit included lots of knives.

into drinking water and food, killing people.

Through their work in the Civil War, doctors gained a better understanding of medical conditions. They discovered proper chemicals to clean their medical instruments. They set up hospitals that kept the sick away from the healthy. Slowly the world of medicine began to improve.

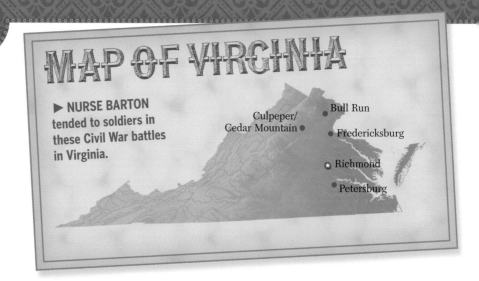

MAP OF VIRGINIA

▶ **NURSE BARTON** tended to soldiers in these Civil War battles in Virginia.

Bull Run

Culpeper/ Cedar Mountain •

• Fredericksburg

◎ Richmond

• Petersburg

nicknamed Clara the "Angel of the Battlefield." She knew her work would be needed for a very long time.

Clara headed back to Washington, D.C., to visit sick soldiers who had arrived in the city. While she was there, she heard the news of more battles in Virginia. Once again, Clara rushed to the scene. When she discovered that some troops hadn't eaten in two days, she built a fire and started cooking. Then she brought the food to the starving troops. Clara and her team moved from battlefield to

◀ **THE ANGEL OF THE BATTLEFIELD** comforted wounded soldiers.

28

battlefield. At the Battle of Antietam on September 17, 1862, Clara removed her first bullet when a soldier begged her to ease his pain. That same day, while Clara held a cup of water to another soldier's parched lips, his body started to shake. Within seconds he was dead. As Clara sadly looked down at the man, she discovered a huge hole in her sleeve. A bullet had ripped right through her dress, lodging in the soldier's body. Clara had narrowly escaped death.

The brave nurse helped soldiers until the end of the Civil War in April 1865. But Clara still didn't rest. Instead, she turned to another important matter—finding missing soldiers.

Mystery PERSON

☞ CLUE 1: I became famous for my nursing work during the Crimean War, when England, France, and Turkey fought against Russia from 1854 to 1856.

☞ CLUE 2: I am known as the founder of modern nursing. I worked hard to improve hospitals in England, where I am from.

☞ CLUE 3: Clara Barton and I wrote a few letters to each other, but we never met in person.

Who am I?

Chapter 7

The American Red Cross Is BORN

Just as the war was ending, families of missing soldiers turned to Clara to help them find their loved ones. Clara got President Lincoln's permission to set up a government office where people could write to look for information about their husbands, brothers, and sons. But when Clara tried to get information from the army, she found nothing. During the war, the army didn't keep records of soldiers lost or missing in battle. So Clara went to

▶ THIS SIGN showed people how to get to the Missing Soldiers Office.

MISSING SOLDIERS. OFFICE. 3RD STORY. ROOM 9. MISS CLARA BARTON

▲ **PRESIDENT ABRAHAM LINCOLN** was a friend—and fan—of Clara Barton.

Annapolis, Maryland, where prisoners of war were brought to recover. As she walked down the streets lined with tents full of soldiers, she tried to get as much information as she could.

Word got out that the Angel of the Battlefield was seeking names of missing men. Soon letters came pouring in. From 1865 to 1868, Clara and her team tracked down information on 22,000 soldiers.

After the Civil War, Clara also traveled around the United States giving speeches. She told people about her experiences in the war. She explained that poor

▲ IN 1865, Clara founded the first national cemetery in Andersonville, Georgia. More than 13,000 Civil War soldiers are buried there.

medical conditions and lack of food and supplies made soldiers suffer even more. People gathered in schools, churches, and theaters to hear her speak.

Off to Europe

Clara was famous overseas as well. While she visited friends in Switzerland in 1869, a man named Dr. Louis Appia came to meet her. He told Clara about a society of thirty-two nations that promised to help wounded soldiers during war. They put up hospital tents in the battlefields and hung a special flag outside each tent. The flag showed a red cross on a white background. The group was known as the International Red Cross.

Clara felt she could help the Red Cross in northern France during the Franco-Prussian War of 1870–1871. She did many of the same jobs there that she had performed in the Civil War. For three years, Clara worked for the International Red Cross. Now she wanted to bring the society to her country.

Bringing It Home

In 1873, an exhausted Clara decided to return to the United States. Her sister Sally, who now lived in New England, had cancer. Clara stayed for six weeks to nurse her. However, Clara didn't like the cold New England winter, so she headed back to Washington, D.C. In the spring, Sally's cancer got worse. Clara hurried back to New England, but Sally died shortly before she got there. Clara went into a depression that lasted for years. She refused to leave her house or talk to people. Clara put aside her dream of bringing the Red Cross to America.

▶ CLARA worked for the International Red Cross in France. An artist drew this picture of her in Europe.

SOLDIERS honored the memories of people who died in the Civil War by holding parades in towns across the United States.

In the spring of 1876, Clara moved to a hospital clinic in Dansville, New York. After a few months of rest, she felt better, so she rented a house in town. The people of Dansville were excited to have a hero there. During the town's Memorial Day parade in 1877, the marchers went to her house and placed flowers at her feet. Clara was touched by their kindness. She remembered that her father had taught her to be loyal to her country. So she decided to go back to work.

For the next four years, Clara worked to start the American Red Cross. She published a letter in newspapers explaining how the group could help during wartime and also during natural disasters. She gave speeches about the importance of the society.

Finally, Clara's hard work and determination paid off. On May 21, 1881, she founded the American Association of the Red Cross in Washington, D.C.

In the fall of that year, terrible forest fires swept through Michigan. The new American Red Cross was ready to help. Clara sent volunteers to the area to hand out food and clothing to the victims and money to help the farmers rebuild lands that had been destroyed.

When the Ohio River flooded in 1884, Clara traveled to the area to review the damage. She saw terrible sights: neighborhoods had been washed away, and piles of rubble were left in their place. Clara and Red Cross volunteers stayed in the flooded area for more than three months to help.

▼ THE AMERICAN RED CROSS raised hundreds of thousands of dollars to help victims of the Johnstown, Pennsylvania, flood in 1889.

The Red Cross also helped out abroad. In 1898, Clara sailed with volunteers to Cuba during the Spanish-American War. They cared for injured American soldiers there. People started to see how important the American Red Cross was.

A New Home

Clara was a generous person who often gave her own money and supplies to those in need. When friends built her a house in Glen Echo, Maryland, Clara turned it into the organization's headquarters.

While Clara was president of the Red Cross, she didn't keep careful track of money and supplies that belonged to the group. Some people accused her of misusing the money. Others said that she was too old to lead it. Clara became very upset. On May 14, 1904, at age eighty-two, she quit as president of the American Red Cross. "The world looks very dark to me," she wrote in her diary shortly after she

◄ CLARA was devoted to her work, but some people didn't trust her business skills.

resigned.

In April 1905, Clara's world got a bit brighter. She helped form the National First Aid Association of America, a group that taught first-aid basics. Clara believed that people who had first-aid skills could help during difficult times. Clara traveled around America teaching people how to treat burns and other skills. In 1909, the group became part of the Red Cross.

Today the American Red Cross stays true to Clara's idea. The group is often first on the scene to rescue people, provide food, or care for the sick. The American Red Cross has helped billions of people around the world—and it all began because of Clara Barton.

Chapter 8

The
FINAL
Battlefield

During her long life, Clara received awards for her work from many nations. She was given the German Iron Cross and the cross of Imperial Russia, among other honors. While the medals were not really important to her, she once joked modestly, "They do brighten up an old dress." In fact, she used to milk cows on the farm with her medals hanging from her clothes.

As Clara grew older, she spent quiet time at home with her

◄ **CLARA** wears one of the many medals that she was awarded during her lifetime.

nephew, Stephen Barton. He took care of his aunt as she grew weak and sick from pneumonia, an illness that attacks the lungs.

On April 10, 1912, Clara dreamed that she was on the battlefield again. She was helping wounded soldiers, cooking meals for troops, and holding the hands of dying men. Clara awoke to tell her doctor about the dream. Then she fell back into a deep sleep. Two days later, ninety-year-old Clara said goodbye to the world with the words, "Let me go, let me go."

Clara was placed in a casket on the steps of her Glen Echo home. Friends, government leaders, and war veterans came to say good-bye. She was buried with her family in Oxford, Massachusetts.

▲ Visitors to Oxford, Massachusetts, can see Clara's grave and tombstone.

Good Works

People can learn about the Angel of the Battlefield and the good works she did through several museums dedicated to her. Clara's home and former Red Cross headquarters in Glen Echo, Maryland, is a National Historic Site. Her birth home in North Oxford,

Visit
GLEN ECHO

Clara Barton lived at her home in Glen Echo, Maryland, for the last fifteen years of her life. In 1906, she wrote, "All seems so home-like, spring-like ... and peaceful that I wonder what can [take] me away again."

Now you can tour Glen Echo and see why Clara loved it so much. In 1975, Congress voted to make the home a National Historic Site. It was the first National Historic Site dedicated to the works— and the life—of a woman. A visit to Glen Echo will take you back one hundred years.

For more information, visit the Glen Echo website: www.nps.gov/clba

Massachusetts, is now the Clara Barton Birthplace Museum. It also serves as a camp for kids and adults with diabetes, continuing her mission to teach and help others. At a time when a woman's place was said to be in the home, Clara Barton was a trailblazer.

Her work in the Civil War and with the Red Cross saved thousands of lives and gave comfort to many more. Her vision as to what the American Red Cross could be, and her determination to create a group she believed in, make Clara Barton a person we still look up to.

Clara's work lives on with the American Red Cross. Millions of people around the United States have been helped by the group. After the terrorist attacks on New York City and Washington, D.C., in 2001, the Red Cross helped with counseling and blood banks. In 2005, hurricanes Katrina and Rita destroyed homes along the Gulf Coast. The Red Cross supplied food and shelter.

It's not likely that Americans were thinking about Clara Barton during these terrible times. But it was because Clara Barton had taken chances, stood up for what she believed, and refused to give up on her dreams that the Red Cross was there.

"The door that nobody else will go in seems always to swing open widely for me."

—CLARA BARTON

Interview

Talking About
CLARA

▲ Bonnie McElveen Hunter

TIME For Kids editor Kathryn Satterfield spoke with Bonnie McElveen Hunter, chairman of the American Red Cross, about Clara Barton.

Q: *How do Clara's beliefs and ideas shape the work the Red Cross does today?*

A: Clara Barton did not look at the color of a person's skin or their uniform when she helped wounded soldiers on both sides during the Civil War. And she believed that disaster victims should be treated fairly, with dignity and compassion. Today's Red Cross volunteers treat everyone with respect, individual care, and concern.

▲ THE RED CROSS is on the scene to help.

Q: *How did Clara help shape aid to people in the United States?*

A: Clara Barton never stayed away from righting a wrong or helping people in need. She did not wait for someone else to solve a problem. When she saw that people needed help during a war or after a disaster, she organized volunteers to provide help. She believed that ordinary people could work together to solve big, serious, or unusual problems.

Q: *Clara was a teacher. How does the Red Cross help to teach people during times of trouble?*

A: To Clara Barton, education was a very important part of the Red Cross's work. Today's American Red Cross organization teaches millions of citizens every year about how to prevent, prepare for, and respond to emergencies. This includes lessons in first aid, water safety, and performing CPR.

▶ AFTER HURRICANE KATRINA, the Red Cross gave out food and water.

Clara Barton's KEY DATES

1821	Born on December 25, in North Oxford, Massachusetts
1833	Begins nursing her brother David
1839	Starts her teaching career in Massachusetts
1854	Moves to Washington, D.C., and works at the U.S. Patent Office
1861	Starts tending wounded Civil War soldiers
1865	Begins searching for missing soldiers
1869	Travels to Europe; learns about the International Red Cross
1881	Forms the American Association of the Red Cross
1904	Resigns as head of the American Red Cross
1912	Dies on April 12, in Glen Echo, Maryland

1836 Texas declares its independence from Mexico; battle at the Alamo takes place.

1868 The typewriter invented.

1912 The "unsinkable" *Titanic* sinks on its first voyage. More than 1,500 drown.